8/13

CR

WITHDRAWN

Ship Shape:
Making Shapes Fly

by Donna Loughran

Content Consultant
David T. Hughes
Mathematics Curriculum Specialist

NORWOOD HOUSE PRESS
Chicago, IL

Norwood House Press
PO Box 316598
Chicago, IL 60631

For information regarding Norwood House Press, please visit our website at
www.norwoodhousepress.com or call 866-565-2900.

Special thanks to: Heidi Doyle
Production Management: Six Red Marbles
Editors: Linda Bullock and Kendra Muntz
Printed in Heshan City, Guangdong, China. 208N—012013

Library of Congress Cataloging–in-Publication Data

Loughran, Donna.

Ship shape: making shapes fly / by Donna Loughran; consultant
David T. Hughes.
p. cm.—(iMath)

Audience: 6–8.
Audience: K to grade 3.
Summary: "The mathematical concepts of naming plane, solid, and composite
shapes are introduced as students enter a spaceship design contest. Readers
learn to identify shapes by counting the sides and corners of flat shapes
and naming the faces of solid shapes. This book includes a discover
activity, an art connection, and a mathematical vocabulary introduction"
—Provided by publisher.

Includes bibliographical references and index.
ISBN: 978-1-59953-554-8 (library edition: alk. paper)
ISBN: 978-1-60357-523-2 (ebook)

1. Geometry, Solid—Juvenile literature. I. Title.
QA491.L68 2012
516.23—dc23
2012034233

CONTENTS

iMath Ideas: Naming Flat and Solid Shapes **6**

Discover Activity: Make a Flying Shape **8**

Get Ready to Rock It! **9**

What's a Rover? **12**

T-Minus 30 and Counting! **14**

Math at Work **15**

Connecting to Art **16**

A Rocket Takes Shape **17**

iMath Ideas: Mission Complete **18**

What Comes Next? **21**

Glossary **22**

Further Reading/Additional Notes **23**

Index **24**

Note to Caregivers:

Throughout this book, many questions are posed to the reader. Some are open-ended and ask what the reader thinks. Discuss these questions with your child and guide him or her in thinking through the possible answers and outcomes. There are also questions posed which have a specific answer. Encourage your child to read through the text to determine the correct answer. Most importantly, encourage answers grounded in reality while also allowing imaginations to soar. Information to help support you as you share the book with your child is provided in the back in the **Additional Notes** section.

Bold words are defined in the glossary in the back of the book.

The Right Shape for the Job

Look around. What shapes do you see? Why do they look the way they do?

Why are wheels round? Why are rockets pointed? Why do boxes have flat sides?

Shapes have different jobs to do. Sometimes, a shape needs to roll. Sometimes, it needs to be fast. Sometimes, it needs to stack.

Keep reading and you will learn a lot more about shapes!

Naming Flat and Solid Shapes

How can you name shapes?

Look at this picture. It shows a happy family. The picture is flat. A flat shape is called a **plane shape**.

How can you name plane shapes?

Idea 1: Count Sides. You can count sides. A **square** has four sides.

Idea 2: Count Corners. You can count corners. Corners are also called **angles**. A **triangle** has three corners, or angles.

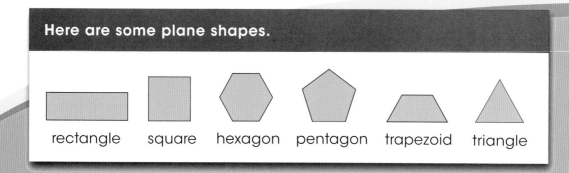

Here are some plane shapes.

rectangle   square   hexagon   pentagon   trapezoid   triangle

Do you think counting sides and corners is a good way to help identify plane shapes?

Solid shapes are not flat. Sometimes, you can pick them up. Or you can walk around them.

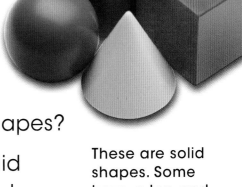

How can you name solid shapes?

Idea 3: Name Faces. All solid shapes have at least one flat side except the sphere. Those flat sides are called **faces**. Each face is a plane shape like a rectangle or circle. For example, a cube has six square faces. Can you see the faces in the solid shapes below?

These are solid shapes. Some have a top and a bottom. Some have sides, too.

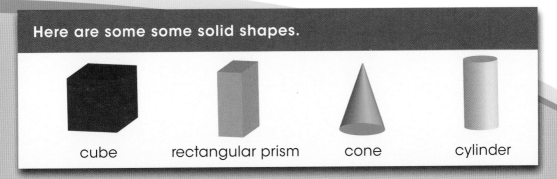

Here are some some solid shapes.

cube   rectangular prism   cone   cylinder

Do you think naming faces is a good way to help identify solid shapes?

Discover Activity

Materials

• paper

Make a Flying Shape

Make a paper airplane. Follow these steps.

1. Fold a piece of paper in half, lengthwise. Then, open the paper.

2. Fold down the top corners to the middle line. The folds will make triangles.

3. Fold down the top corners again. The folds will make triangles again.

4. Fold both sides in. These are the wings.

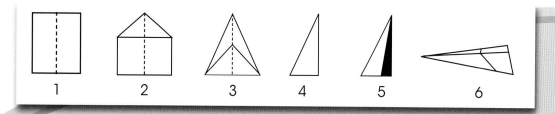

5. Start at the pointed end. Fold one wing back. This forms a triangle. Do this for both sides.

6. Hold the airplane with its wings up. Let it fly!

Now, change the shape of your airplane. Fly it again. Does anything change? Does the new shape fly farther?

Get Ready to Rock It!

"Did you see the poster?" Callie says. She and some friends are in the lunchroom. "The poster tells about a contest. Anyone can enter. It looks really fun."

"Is it a sport?" Henry asks. "I'm good at soccer. I can kick a ball high in the air!"

"Well, air is important in the contest," Callie answers.

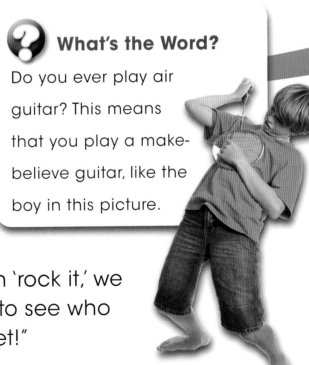

❓ What's the Word?

Do you ever play air guitar? This means that you play a make-believe guitar, like the boy in this picture.

Amanda says, "Is it an air guitar contest? Does the team that rocks win?"

Callie giggles. "If we can 'rock it,' we may win! The contest is to see who can build the best rocket!"

Callie says, "The contest is for teams of four people. There are four of us. But we need a teacher to help us."

The team reads the poster again. Mr. Barton, the science teacher, sees them. He asks, "Do you want to join the contest?"

Amanda says, "Yes, Mr. Barton. Will you work with us?"

Mr. Barton answers without smiling, "You make a good team. I'm excited about this contest, too.

Let's meet again tomorrow. We can talk it over then."

"Do you think Mr. Barton is really excited? I can't tell for sure," says Henry.

Callie shrugs her shoulders. "I can't tell," she says.

Read the contest rules on the next page. Would you want to be on a team?

Blast into the Future!

Spaceship Design Contest
Citywide Team Challenge for Elementary Students

Rules

Each team must have four members. Members must be in the same grade.

A teacher or other adult must help the team.

The design must have both flat shapes and solid shapes.

The design must be creative.

Each team must write a paragraph about their spaceship.

Each team must draw a picture of their spaceship.

Teams may use any materials to build their spaceship.

What's a Rover?

The team meets Mr. Barton the next morning. "I have some pictures I want to show you," Mr. Barton says. "I thought they might give you some ideas."

The team looks at the pictures. Henry points to one and asks, "That's a **rover**, isn't it?"

Mr. Barton nods his head. "Yes, it is, Henry."

Henry looks at his friends. "Rovers are machines. They roll across a planet. Scientists decide where the rover goes."

"The rovers pick up soil and rocks," Henry explains. "They send information to Earth. We could make one!"

What shapes do you see in this rover?

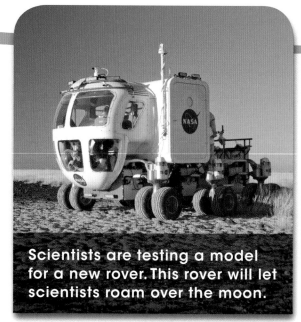

Scientists are testing a model for a new rover. This rover will let scientists roam over the moon.

"This is a rover, too!" Callie says. She points to a picture. "It looks like something in a movie!"

Mr. Barton smiles. "I guess it does. But it's real."

Chris says, "It looks like an insect. Look at all of its shapes."

Look at the picture. What plane and solid shapes do you see in this rover?

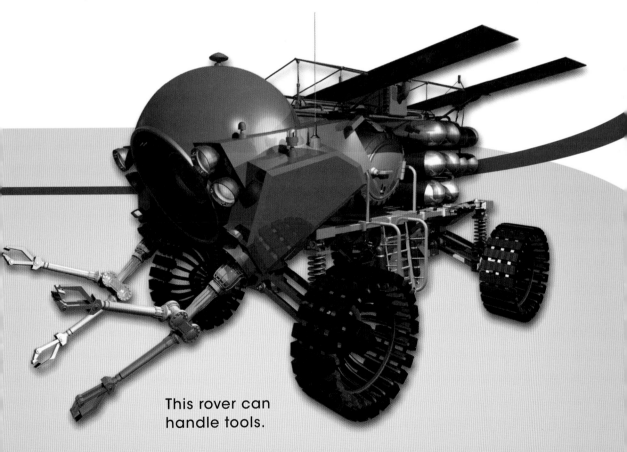

This rover can handle tools.

"We have 30 days to make our spaceship," says Amanda. "Maybe we should build a rocket. All we would need is cardboard. Cardboard is strong. It's lightweight and bendable, too," she says.

The team agrees. They begin to draw designs. They practice making shapes.

"I want to paint the rocket, too," Callie says.

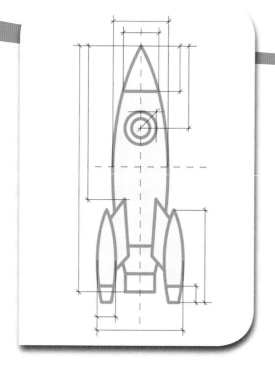

Team members draw pictures of what their spaceship might look like. What shapes do you see in their drawing?

Math at Work

Who designs real spaceships? Engineers do. Their designs follow these rules:

1. The spaceship must be able to hold scientists and the materials they need for their work.

2. The spaceship must be easy to make and to keep running.

3. A spaceship must have as few stages as possible. A stage is a rocket engine. It burns fuel to move a spaceship through space. When the fuel is gone, the stage falls away.

4. A spaceship must be used more than once.

5. Finally, the spaceship must pass every safety test.

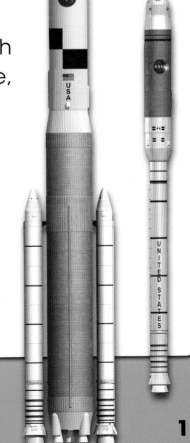

One day, rockets like these could carry people to the Earth's Moon and to Mars.

Connecting to Art

Many artists think about what life might be like in space. They draw and paint pictures of space cities.

Artists use shapes in their art. They put shapes together to make a **composite** (kuhm-PAWS-it). A composite is a shape made from two or more shapes.

Look at the drawing above. It is filled with shapes. Some are composite shapes. What shapes do you see?

A Rocket Takes Shape

The team works hard to make different shapes. They want the right shapes for a rocket.

First, they make the rocket's body. It is a composite shape. It has two shapes. What are they?

Next, they use a round shape to make legs for the rocket. What is the shape?

They cut the round shape into four **equal** parts. That means that each part is the same size.

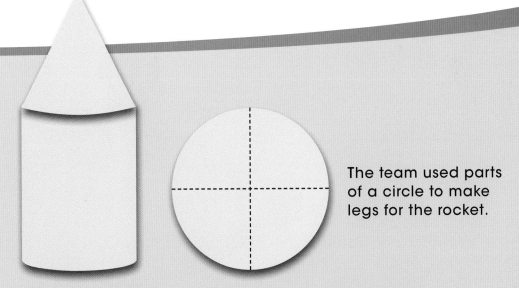

The team used parts of a circle to make legs for the rocket.

The team keeps building until the rocket is complete.

Henry smiles and says, "It's finally finished! Our rocket looks like the design I made."

"It looks great!" Amanda says. "It's really colorful!"

"We have used lots of shapes," Chris says. "Some are plane shapes and some are solid shapes. How can we name the plane shapes?"

Idea 1: Count Sides. "We can count the number of sides they have," Callie says.

Idea 2: Count Corners. Henry says, "We can count the number of corners, too."

What plane shapes does the rocket have?

The team painted their rocket. They used extra cardboard to make the moon's surface. They put a toy astronaut on the ground next to their rocket. Henry made a drawing of it.

"Now we need to check the solid shapes," says Amanda. "Solid shapes have faces. Their faces are plane shapes. If we name the plane shapes, it will help us identify the solid shapes."

Idea 3: Name Faces. "We can count sides and corners to help us name the faces," Chris says. "Then, we can use those flat shapes to find out what solid shapes we have."

What solid shapes does the rocket have?

 What's the Word?

Have you ever wondered what it would be like to walk among the stars? In 1806, Jane Taylor wrote a poem called "Twinkle, Twinkle, Little Star." Do you ever sing the first part of this poem?

Twinkle, twinkle, little star,
How I wonder what you are!
Up above the world so high,
Like a diamond in the sky.

It is finally the day of the contest and the team enters their rocket.

Chris, Amanda, Henry, and Callie earn first prize! They all smile for pictures. Then, Amanda says to the judges, "We have something else to show you! Follow us outside."

Mr. Barton helps the team set up their rocket. The students step away as he sets the rocket off. It flies several feet. Then, it falls softly back to Earth.

The judges cheer. And the team laughs as Mr. Barton jumps up and down.

Chris says, "Mr. Barton is excited now! I'm glad we worked together to design our own spaceship!"

What Comes Next?

Make a model of a rocket or a rover. Think about what you want the rocket or rover to do. Then, think about which shapes work best for each job. Draw your design.

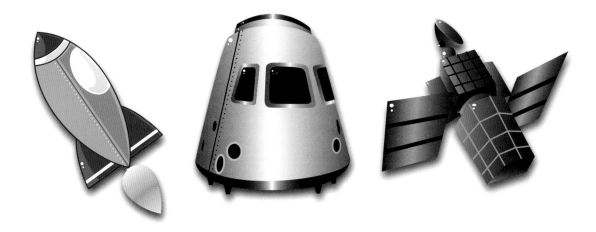

Play with paper or cardboard shapes. Fold or cut them and see what shapes you can make.

Use glue and tape to keep your shapes together. Decorate your rocket or rover with markers or paint.

Now you are ready for an outer space adventure!

GLOSSARY

angle(s): a corner on a shape where two lines meet.

composite: a shape that is made of two or more shapes.

equal: the same as.

faces: the flat sides of a solid shape.

plane shape: a flat shape. You can measure the length and the width of plane shapes.

rover: a machine that is used to explore planets.

solid shapes: shapes with faces. You can measure the length, the width, and the height of solid shapes.

square: a plane shape with four sides and four corners. The four sides are the same length.

triangle: a plane shape with three sides and three corners.

FURTHER READING

FICTION

Oliver, the Spaceship, and Me, by Lynn Rowe Reed, Holiday House, 2009

Robot Zot!, by John Scieszka, Simon and Schuster Books for Young Readers, 2009

NONFICTION

Captain Invincible and the Space Shapes, by Stuart J. Murphy, Harper Collins, 2001

Museum Shapes, by The Metropolitan Museum of Art, Little, Brown Books for Young Readers, 2005

Additional Notes

The page references below provide answers to questions asked throughout the book. Questions whose answers will vary are not addressed.

Page 12: The front has windows with four sides. They look almost like rectangles and trapezoids. The space in the middle looks like a rectangular prism. The face in front of the prism is like a rectangle. The sign on the rectangle side is a circle. There is another circle on the front of the rover. The pole looks like a cylinder. The wheels are circles.

Page 13: Some possible answers may include: The arms and poles between the wheels are cylinders. The wheels are circles. The wings are rectangles. The body is a solid shape.

Page 14: Caption question: Students may say they see shapes resembling cones, trapezoids, rectangles, and circles.

Page 16: Some possible answers may include: The houses are flat composite shapes. They are made of rectangles, triangles, squares, and trapezoids. There are circles in the sky and on the planet. The spaceship has circle windows and a triangle tail.

Page 17: The body is made of a cylinder and a cone. The round shape is a circle.

Page 18: There are rectangles and circles on the rocket and on the ladder. The flag is a rectangle. There are circles on the ground.

Page 19: Its body is a cylinder with a cone on top. The flagpole is a cylinder. The surface that the rocket sits on is a rectangular prism.

INDEX

angle(s), 6

composite, 16–17

equal, 17

faces, 7, 19

plane shape, 6–7, 18–19

rover, 12–13, 21

solid shapes, 7, 11, 13, 19

square, 6–7

triangle, 6, 8

Content Consultant

David T. Hughes

David is an experienced mathematics teacher, writer, presenter, and adviser. He serves as a consultant for the Partnership for Assessment of Readiness for College and Careers. David has also worked as the Senior Program Coordinator for the Charles A. Dana Center at The University of Texas at Austin and was an editor and contributor for the *Mathematics Standards in the Classroom* series.